Geoff Thompson's Ground Fighting Series

Pins: The Bedrock

Geoff Thompson

SUMMERSDALE

Summersdale Publishers Ltd
46 West Street
Chichester
West Sussex
PO19 1RP
United Kingdom

www.summersdale.com

Printed and bound in Great Britain.

ISBN 1 84024 171 3

Photographs by Paul Raynor

Important note

With ground fighting techniques the author recommends that you practice only under supervision to avoid accidents and always employ the 'tap system' in practice (if you want to submit or a technique is too painful or you wish to stop practice at any time tap the mat, tap yourself or your opponent with your hand or foot; if this is not possible just say to your opponent 'tap'). If an opponent taps out it is imperative that you release your hold immediately or suffer the consequence of what might be serious injury, and remember, what goes around comes around. If you do not release when he taps he may not release the next time you tap.

About the author

Geoff Thompson has written over 20 published books and is known world wide for his autobiography *Watch My back*, about his nine years working as a night club doorman. He holds the rank of 6th Dan black belt in Japanese karate, 1st Dan in Judo and is also qualified to senior instructor level in various other forms of wrestling and martial arts. He has several scripts for stage, screen and TV in development with Destiny Films.

He has published several articles for GQ magazine, and has also been featured in *FHM*, *Maxim*, *Arena*, *Front* and *Loaded* magazines, and has been featured many times on mainstream TV.

Geoff is currently a contributing editor for *Men's Fitness* magazine.

For full details of other books and videos by
Geoff Thompson, visit www.geoffthompson.com

ACKNOWLEDGEMENTS

With special thanks to Marc McFann and my good friend and grappling sempai Rick Young.

Contents

Introduction

As I sit and write this text about Ground Fighting, I fondly look back on nearly 25 wonderful years of training in the martial arts, about 15 of those years as the instructor of one of the best, certainly toughest and definitely friendliest clubs in Great Britain.

Sadly, only yesterday I taught my last lesson to what was only a spattering of loyal students. It was a sad day for me with only a handful of people around me, whom I had grown to love and respect, there to see the end.

For the last 15 years I have put my heart and soul into my club only to see, on this final day, the emaciated remnants of what was once a feared battle ground where strong characters were tempered and the faint of heart feared to tread.

I won't go on about it, that's not what you have bought this book to read about, only to say that . . . well . . . there's nothing much more to say really, other than the fact that, for me it's the end of an era.

Many people have written, or spoken to me over the years about coming to Coventry to train at my master class but for whatever reason few seemed to make it so I decided to write a series of books and put together a series of videos on the type of lessons one could expect to receive had the journey been made.

The series is now even more apt because I no longer have a club and, unless you manage to make it down to one of the few seminars that I teach each year, this will be the only way you'll get to train with me.

With this in mind I write, as I taught, only about the things I actually train in myself. I will not, I can assure you, use superfluous technique to fill a book. There will be different genres of book according to the range/ryu that I am writing about, this series being the wonderful and exciting ground fighting range.

When you consider the fact that 95% of all fights go to ground and yet probably only 5% of martial artists are adequately prepared, or address ground fighting, something seems acutely amiss.

Pins: The Bedrock

Hopefully this series will redress the balance and prepare the latter, whilst at the same time adding information and knowledge to the curriculum of those that are already in the know.

I have to say, that of all the systems that I have studied over the years ground fighting has been the most in-depth and demanding, though by its outer shell it may not appear so; only the very strong will go the full course and become proficient.

I have been lucky enough to train in several systems that incorporate ground fighting as their main range, Judo, Ju-Jitsu, Wrestling etc, and whilst all are very strong each has its own particular weakness. What I intend to do with these books is include the best of these systems and add, where appropriate, the now illegal techniques that were banned to make them safer to practice or more commercially, socially, Olympically acceptable.

I have no love for sport budo - though I do admire the great sports men that we have produced in this country - and I am not worried about being commercially or socially acceptable - I'll paint it as I see it.

I know from experience that it is the 'illegal', ugly techniques that make a system potent and workable in a society that no longer holds the martial artist in any esteem.

Whilst I am a great grappling fan and firmly believe that the grappler is potentate when rules are not in play, I have to state categorically that the ground is still the last place to be in a real fight. If you are in a match fight, as opposed to a 3 second fight or an ambush fight, the ground can be a safe option because you only have the one opponent to deal with.

However, match fighting is a lost art that only the very courageous seek; the enemy of today is a cowardly team fighter who works under the umbrella of deception, and whilst you might be capable of eating him alive on the ground it doesn't stop his mates kicking your face in or his girl friend stabbing you whilst your hands are tied up with your prostrate opponent.

A good puncher, one who understands the enemy and understands himself, will finish 95% of his fights from punching range and will be at home having his supper when his opponent is still coming around in some puddle in suburbia.

Pins: The Bedrock

Having said that, some of the best punchers on the planet still end up on the floor because they do not understand enough about themselves or their enemy (see 3 Second Fighter) to employ their punching prowess to good effect. The kickers, unfortunately, fare even worse and end up on their backs more than the only whore in a town full of sex starved men on pay day.

Having pointed out the weaknesses of going to ground, I think it's important to point out that the confidence one develops from fighting on the ground is second to none. After all, the worst case scenario in a real fight is ending up on the floor; if you are good at fighting from the floor you become more confident and committed in the vertical ranges because, if you do find worst case scenario and the fight hits the deck, so what, you're good there too.

I believe that ground fighting will find a re-birth and people will realise what I have been saying for the last 15 years, that if you can't fight on the ground then you are not a complete fighter.

For those that are perceptive enough to see that this series of books will be of enormous help, they will teach you that anyone can be beaten on the ground, big or small, as long as you have the knowledge. Most fighters run out of steam very quickly in a real fight, especially when it hits the ground, and what may have been a vertical monster is often a horizontal mouse. How you hit the floor is out of the context of this book, and series, though my books Real Grappling and Dead Or Alive cover a lot of good practical take downs. In this series we are dealing with what to do when you are down there.

There are different schools of thought about whether one should stay on the ground, once down, or get back up at the earliest opportunity. This depends largely on the circumstances and quite often you have no choice in the matter anyway. By strategically placing yourself in certain pins you do often have the opportunity to get back to your feet, and if that opportunity arises it is usually wise to snatch it with both hands, especially if you are dealing with more than one opponent.

The Match fight is slightly different - you are only fighting with one person and you may have taken him to the ground because he was too strong for you on his feet. If this is the case and he feels weaker on the ground then stay there and finish, there's no sense in letting a vertical monster back to his feet again. After all, if the guy is a hardened fighter he'll be glad to take the finishing kicks you throw just to get back to his feet again. Just

Pins: The Bedrock

because you are vertical and he is horizontal is no guarantee of victory. As I said earlier, often the most frightening of opponents in vertical fighting is an absolute mouse on the floor because he has no experience of that range.

Look at the great white shark, the most feared killer of the seas, unequivocally the king of the deep waters - how do the deep sea divers deal with them? By using electrical waves that frighten the sharks and scare them away. The only reason it's effective is because the sensation is outside of the shark's experience and they do not know how to deal with it.

Taking a vertical fighter to the ground is, in effect, doing the same thing - taking them outside of their experience. One of my younger students, Matty, had a situation about one month ago with a very reputable street fighter from one of the rougher parts of Coventry. My student is 17 years old and about 11 stone, his opponent, P, was 26 and 15 and a half stone.

Matty was out with a couple of his friends when P approached and started an argument with them. They were all pretty scared because they knew this guy, he had a huge reputation as being a heavy weight in the area. P started bullying one of the lads who didn't really want any trouble, when he tried to tell P this he got knocked out for his impertinence. Everyone stood back,

'ANY ONE ELSE WANT SOME?' P shouted, not expecting anyone to take him up on the challenge.

'Yeah, I'll have a bit,' replied Matty.

He'd been involved in several hundred animal day fights at my club and figured that it couldn't be any worse than that.

'You gotta be **cking joking, I'll kill ya',' came the bemused reply.

'Give it your best shot!' Matty said, stepping forward.

The fight was on.

A few punches were thrown and a clinch quickly ensued, as is the way with most match fights. Matty managed to reach P's leg and they tumbled to the ground where he held P in a tight scarf hold, for a few seconds P went crazy trying to escape the hold but he was held with a vice-like grip.

Pins: The Bedrock

Matty could tell that P was tiring, in fact he was wheezing so much at one stage that Matty thought he had asthma. While he held P in the scarf hold Matty fired a couple of punches and head butts into his face and then jumped straight into the mount position (to be detailed later) where he continued to fire pummelling punches into P's face.

In a desperate bid to escape P turned over onto his belly, which is where Matty wanted him to turn, and Matty quickly wrapped a strangle around his neck. P struggled frantically for a couple of seconds before falling unconscious.

The whole fight lasted 10 seconds. After five minutes P came around, it was twenty minutes before he knew where he was and two weeks before he would venture out of his flat and show his face again.

The important thing in this true story is not so much the finish, although that is important, but rather it is the way that Matty, three stone lighter than his opponent, controlled his opponent with pins until he was ready for the finish.

That is what this first volume is about, perfecting the pins so that you can control the opponent right from the off. It would be very easy at this point to rush off into the histrionics of advanced finishing techniques like strangles and bars but they are useless without the correct base of pinning techniques - please don't rush ahead and try to run before you can walk because, when the shit hits the fan and you find yourself in a real fight and on the ground, the finishing techniques will fail you because you have no foundation; so, don't put the gloss on your woodwork until you have rubbed it down and applied the primer, in this case, the pins.

What I'll do to start is isolate the main pins and then, later in the book, show you how to move around the body from one pin to another so that you can always work away from your opponent's strength and, eventually, move into a good finishing position. I will also detail how to defend and drill the pins. An excellent place to finish is the mount position and wherever you are on the ground the mount is always accessible.

When you first start practising the pins with a partner, do so with compliancy so that you can learn the correct technique. Once this has been attained practice full out, with no partner compliancy, so that you develop the correct muscles to defend the pin.

Pins: The Bedrock

Out of all the six books in this series, this one will be the most important, even though it may be the most basic, because it is the bedrock of everything else that you learn.

When you build a house it needs first and foremost to be on a firm foundation and your foundation with ground fighting is the pins.

Chapter One

The Mount Position

The mount is very often called the 'school boy position', because it's the position you always seemed to end up in when you fought in the school playground. As it is seen as synonymous with school boy fighting, it's devastating potency is often missed, and some (the uninitiated) even laugh at the mount as though it is infantile. These people have obviously never been below the mount or they would not be so quick to scoff. In my opinion it is probably the strongest and most powerful of all the pins, certainly once you have learned to defend it, and can be sought very quickly from all the other pinning positions.

From the mount one can finish with the 'bread and butter' punches and strikes or the intricate, and yet paradoxically simple, bars and chokes. You can either punch the opponent out or punch him until he turns onto his stomach and then choke him out. If he feeds you an arm as a means of defence to your blows, you can bar and break it off; if you so desire you are also in a very good position to get back to your feet, whilst your opponent is still horizontal, and finish with kicking/stamping techniques. You are also in the enviable position of being able

Pins: The Bedrock

to punch your opponent whilst he cannot reach your face to punch back, and thus you have the leverage while he does not. Whilst it is conventional to mount on the opponent's belly you can also, if he turns slightly, mount him on his side, or if he turns completely mount him on his back.

These are the different mounts:

Belly Mount

Sit astride the opponent with your knees wide to spread your weight and thus make it harder for him to escape. You can either sit upright (a good punching position), or lean forward with your palms on the ground as base.

Pins: The Bedrock

Side Mount

If the opponent turns slightly to his side you may mount his side. The opponent is far more open to attacking blows from here because his arms are redundant as defending tools. Again you may sit upright to attack or forward with your palms on the ground to base.

Back Mount

If the opponent turns completely onto his belly, usually in a bid to escape, you may mount his back, upright for attacking or forward for basing. From this position he is very vulnerable to attacks from your elbows and the finishing choke or strangle.

Pins: The Bedrock

Firstly, get as comfortable as possible with these positions, using partner compliancy to perfect technique. Once a comfort level has been found, move onto defending the mount. Usually (certainly for the first few seconds of taking up the mount, or any pin for that matter) the opponent will panic and start to buck and thrash in a bid to escape. You must expect this or you'll lose the pin as quick as you found it. He will get a surge of in-fight adrenalin (see Fear book) that, for a few seconds, will make him very strong, certainly strong enough to throw you from a strong to a vulnerable position.

Adrenalin is like a bodily turbo drive and whilst it will make him very strong for a few seconds it will also eat away his fuel at the same rate, so ride the storm until he is knackered - then he's just a punch bag. This is especially so when dealing with unfit fighters (most of them are very unfit). When I fight on the ground I often spark my opponent's in-fight adrenalin by inflicting pain-punch, bite, elbow, etc., in order to empty his fuel tanks. Beware though; if you use this ploy remember what you are doing and the effect that it may have: you're giving him a few seconds of dynamic energy that will throw you from your pin if you are not prepared for it. So remember to ride the storm until his fuel tanks are empty.

The most vulnerable time for a pin is when you first take it and when you go for a finish - these are the times that most people forget to defend their hold. The second that you put a pin on someone they will try to fight out of it, because their brain senses danger and releases in-fight adrenalin to assist. Similarly when you give an opponent pain his brain will release in-fight adrenalin to act as both anaesthesia to the pain and fuel to the escape, and it's the same thing when you go for a finish. His brain will sense that the end is near and initiate fight or flight that will enable him to buck and thrash ferociously for a few seconds. Rather than fight biceps against biceps, will against will, go with the flow and ride the opponent like a bucking horse, if you try to meet force with force you'll get as tired as he - and if he's stronger, you may lose.

Defending the Mount

There are two main positions from the mount (as illustrated), one used primarily as an attacking position and the other primarily as a defending position.

The attack position is high with the hands cocked ready to attack, the defence position low, almost lying on the opponent with your hands/arms spread out in front to use as a base. The hands and feet can be used to base out and stop the opponent escaping,

Pins: The Bedrock

the hands directly to the side and in front, the feet directly to the side and behind. The feet may also be intertwined with the opponent's to further secure a good solid base. At any appropriate time in the mount the head, teeth, elbow, etc., can be used to attack and finish (or turn) the mounted opponent. Again, this is real bread and butter stuff and should be perfected before moving on to more technical finishes.

The following are techniques to help you defend the mount. You need no partner compliancy here though you can start at 50% (the person under the mount trying to escape using only 50% of his energy) and work up to all out.

The first lesson to learn here is if the opponent moves his hands away from his face, to try and push you off, whack him in the face to discourage him. If he moves his hands away from his face then, logically, his face is unguarded and should be attacked at once. As an automatic reaction he will then bring his hands back to his face as a means of defence (in practice you may use open hand to attack to save serious injury).

Swimming technique

If the opponent tries to push you off with his hands on your chest hold your mount and swim (in a breast stroke kind of motion) through his arms with both your arms. Be forceful and break his grip; as you swim through, hit the opponent in the face to discourage him from trying again and then base your hands out in front of you.

Pins: The Bedrock

Left & Right Base (Basing)

What to do if the opponent does manage to get his hands to your chest and push over to your right, or left, or if he bridges (arches his hips to throw you off) to try and get you off. As he bridges or pushes you, reach over and base with the appropriate hand (left if to the left side, right if to the right). If for some reason one of your hands is tied up and you cannot base to that side you may use the leg of that side to base instead.

Pins: The Bedrock

Rear Base

If you find yourself being bridged or pushed directly forward, use both hands to base behind the opponent's head.

Grapevining

For an opponent who is particularly aggressive, you can grapevine your feet around his ankles, making it near impossible for him to bridge or push you off. The only problem with grapevining is that it can also disable you from being mobile, and although you have tied up your opponent, in a way you have also tied up yourself. Push your feet on the inside of the opponent's legs and wrap them around his ankles. For better control straighten yours, and thus his, legs. Once he has calmed down a little you may release his legs so that you can continue with the job in hand.

Pins: The Bedrock

Riding the mount

Most often the opponent in the mount will try and roll over onto his stomach in a bid to escape; he will innately feel that this is the 'safe' (if not the only) escape route, even though it is probably the worst position possible when dealing with a good ground fighter. If the opponent is strong and intent on turning and you do not allow him room between your legs to do so, he may catch your leg as he turns and turn you over with him as he escapes.

So if he tries to escape by turning, offer token resistance by tensing your thighs. This is to make out that you do not want him to turn, and as he tries harder relax your thighs and allow him the tiniest of margins between your legs to turn. As he turns you can place him straight in a choke or strangle. This is called riding the mount.

To practice, have the opponent roll to his left several times, as he does so you ride the mount using your hands to base and keep balance, and on his last roll apply the choke. Then get the opponent to roll the opposite way several times and repeat the exercise. Please bear in mind that, in a real situation, whenever the head presents itself it is open for undefended, pummelling strikes; this will be your base and most important finishers.

Attacking from the mount

To practice attacking from the mount, have the opponent wear a pair of focus mitts and hold them by either side of his head, then punch the pads with all the power you can muster. This is an acquired technique that must be practised because it is not the same as punching from a standing position. As you drive the punch home, twist your arm into the technique. Alternatively you can hold one of the opponent's hands and punch the other or head butt the pads instead of using your fists.

Pins: The Bedrock

The mount is probably the best pin for control and for finishing. Many hours must be spent learning to defend this position or, as I have already said, it will be lost as quickly as it is found.

Chapter Two

Side Four Quarter Hold Down

The side 4 1/4 is an excellent controlling pin and, once perfected, easy to maintain. It also offers some excellent finishing techniques to the advanced ground fighter and one can move to the mount or the upper 4 1/4 from here very easily. In many ways it is a traveller's rest hold; that is you can take a rest here when needed and allow an aggressive opponent to thrash himself out. It takes very little energy to defend, though a tremendous amount of energy to escape from. Personally I use this hold as a stop gap when travelling to my finishing position in the mount.

Side 4 1/4 Hold down

Lie across the opponent's torso with your legs straight and spread eagled behind you and your hands basing on the floor in front.

Broken side 4 1/4 Hold down

You can break the hold by tying off the opponent's leg with one of your arms and/or by placing your arm (arm nearest to the opponent's head) around the opponent's head. These variations help to control the opponent better but can often end up in a battle of strength that will leave you, as well as the opponent, tired.

Side 4 1/4 Hold down - knees up

Whilst the base hold has the legs straight and splayed you can also, if you require, bring the knees up to the side of the opponent's body for tighter control. This is also handy if you wish to try and stand up or move to a different pin/position. Whilst it is harder for the opponent to escape whilst your legs are splayed and straight it is also harder for you to move and/or finish.

Pins: The Bedrock

Defending the side 4 1/4 Hold down

Sensitivity is imperative here - the JKD and Wing Chun stylists should come into their own when defending the mounts. The basic premise when fighting on the ground, (actually when fighting in general), is not to fight force with force. If I have pinned the opponent and he moves to the right in a bid to escape, then I will move with him as opposed to against him; if I use my strength against his then I will get just as tired as him or if he is stronger than I (very unlikely let me tell you) then I will lose the hold. So I will not try and block his strength; rather I will use it.

If he pushes to the right I will follow using minimal movement. As much as I can I will let him take me the way he is moving, he'll be moving my weight as well as his own and thus get tired twice as quickly. If he moves to the left I will do the same and move to the left with him, or if he pushes forward or backward then I will move forward or backward, all the time leaning my weight on him to make his task harder and his movement more laboured. To help me do this I will keep my legs straight and push up onto the balls of my feet focusing all of my weight onto and through my chest and into his chest. I will 'feel' (the feel comes with much "flight time") his movement and go with it, without opposing it - when he gets tired I'll go for my finish.

If I want to drain his energy quicker, or psyche him out, I'll bite his belly/chest/arm etc. (whatever is available), and give him an injection of in-fight adrenalin. If he goes crazy for a few seconds then I'll ride the storm until his energy is all spent, then I'll finish - if it psyches him and he bottles out then he's finished anyway.

Tying up

In his bid to escape the opponent will try everything and anything. In my bid to hold the pin I will make things as awkward and painful and uncomfortable as I can by tying up his arms, biting, punching his exposed groin (for want of a better expression) and/or leaning my elbow/forearm on his exposed neck and throat, etc.

This hold is one of the easiest to maintain and hardest to escape from; flight time (time spent practising the move) is the essential pre-requisite to its effectiveness.

Chapter Three

The Scarf Hold

Probably the most recognisable of all the pins is the scarf hold; this is also the hold that many street fighters innately secure to win or control a situation that hits the floor. Whilst it is a relatively simple technique to hold, it is a very difficult position to escape from - though there are several good methods (see Vol. Two: Escapes). Like the side 4 1/4 it is a strong hold that lends itself well to finishing techniques and to movement to other pins - specifically the mount. The opponent held in scarf hold is highly vulnerable to illegal techniques like biting, gouging, punching, etc.

The Scarf Hold

Place your right arm (may be reversed if working at the opposite side of the body) around the opponent's neck (he is lying on his back) and grabbing either his clothing or your own right knee to secure, place his left arm under your right armpit and bring your right knee close to his face whilst your left leg splays out, hurdler style, behind you, keeping the knee on the floor.

Pins: The Bedrock

Bend forward and keep your head as close to the opponent's as possible; this will protect your throat, face and eyes from his free left hand. This leaves your right hand free to attack the opponent. If the opponent brings his free left hand over to attack you lift your head up, grab the hand and bend back the fingers and push it under your chin.

If his right hand gets free from under your left arm, you can do one of several things:

1) Bar it over your right leg.

Pins: The Bedrock

2) If the arm will not straighten, switch legs to create a higher fulcrum and bar it over your left leg.

3) If he is still struggling then quickly switch back the legs and drive the arm into/over the lower fulcrum of the right leg.

Pins: The Bedrock

4) Tie the arm off under the reverse/left leg, to bar turn your hips up to the ceiling and push.

5) Tie the arm off under the right leg.

Pins: The Bedrock

6) If the opponent uses the freed arm to try and push or punch your face, quickly move your face away and push the arm with your left arm so that his arm is trapped across his own neck; this, when squeezed, will make for a strong choke/strangle.

Defending the Scarf Hold

Defending this hold is very similar to defending any hold, i.e., go with the flow, if the opponent pulls you around to the left then go to the left with him, if he pulls you around to the right then go to the right, so that he is getting tired and you're getting carried. If the opponent is getting a little too frisky then jab your thumb into his eye, that ought to quieten him down a little.

This hold is only difficult to defend when you are restricted (no gouging, punching, biting etc.). If there are no restrictions (in a real fight there certainly are none) and if the opponent is too strong then an eye gouge will be the end of the fight - if you so desire. If he brings his free arm into play he really has no target, other than the bony part of your head that will hurt him as much as you, but, as stated earlier, that can be tied off any way.

If he frees his other arm it can be dealt with as per foregoing illustrations. If the opponent is really strong and you are struggling to hold him you can roll slightly onto your belly and bring your right leg behind you (this is almost the Jack-knife position) to spread the weight, but this is really changing holds as opposed to defending a specific hold.

Pins: The Bedrock

Attacking the Scarf Hold

We've already mentioned a little about attacking from the scarf hold by using gouging techniques; this is without doubt the strongest and most brutal attack from this position.

However, not everyone has the inclination to gouge an opponent's eye out: more affable alternatives may be biting his exposed nose/face (no!), pushing your fist or fingers into the side of his wind pipe, or even sticking your fingers up his nostrils and tearing.

To be honest most of it is pretty ugly stuff, but, if the guy is going to take your life or rape your wife they are handy to know.

A lot of punching power, contrary to popular belief, can be generated from the scarf hold position. The best way to practice is to get the opponent to wear a pair of focus mitts and hold them, from underneath the hold, close to his head, then you hit them.

Again, this is an acquired technique that will need much practice before real power can be generated, but with practice these punches are/can be very powerful finishing techniques.

Pins: The Bedrock

Practising this hold, and all the pins, will develop manipulative strength and also the ability to hold an opponent with minimal strength so as not to over tax your reserves. So practice with as little compliancy as possible, eventually with no compliancy at all.

Chapter Four

The Jack-Knife

The Jack-knife is a sort of in-between hold that I invented (I'm sure that other people have found the same hold - but I've never seen it in any books or on any videos before so as far as I'm concerned, it's mine) and is a wonderful little hold that takes you nicely from scarf hold to upper 4 1/4. It also works very nicely in conjunction with scarf hold either to help hold the base or finish with a smother hold (smothering is another concept that I'm sure others have found but I have never seen written about before, so that's mine as well).

The Jack-knife

Basically the jack-knife controls the opponent's head at a 45 degree angle to his body; somewhere (anywhere) between scarf hold and upper 4 1/4 hold. Take the hold from the scarf hold position so the opponent's right arm is still tucked under your left armpit. Your right arm is still wrapped around the opponent's neck, bring your left arm forward to either pin the head still or push it, via any pain or pressure point, so that the opponent's mouth and nose are towards the ceiling.

Pins: The Bedrock

This will place him ideally for the smother (the smother is when you cover the opponent's mouth and nose with any part of your body, in this case the shoulder and upper chest, and lean/press your weight on them to block the airways and stop them breathing). It can also be used as a traveller's rest if you want to take a minute out and think about what's going on. Also to allow the opponent to tire himself out a little; the body is very open to pummelling punches which can be used to disable or inflict in-fight adrenalin, and the eyes are also very vulnerable to gouging with your right hand.

Broken Jack-knife

This hold can be performed broken by lying across the opponent's face with the hands free (as illus) to base.

Pins: The Bedrock

Knees up

If the opponent is strong it is advisable to keep the legs straight and splayed, stay on your toes; as he tires you can shorten the hold by bringing the knees up closer to the opponent's face to prepare for finish or to get back to your feet.

Defending the Jack-knife

As with all defences stay loose and go with the flow, move in the same direction as the opponent, let him take you as opposed to making big movements yourself. Keep on your toes if he is strong and make sure that he feels your weight. If you find that he is too strong and you cannot hold him then move to a better pin, an upper 4 1/4 or mount.

Chapter Five

Reverse Scarf Hold

The reverse scarf hold is an ideal resting position when one is travelling around the body, especially from upper 4 1/4 to mount. It can also be a very strong hold and, if you get a good grip of the opponent's neck and head, one can crank the neck and finish from here. More realistically it is a very good traveller's rest hold.

Reverse scarf hold

Sitting at the head of the opponent, facing the same direction wrap your left arm under his head and around his neck, under from the left side of his head and out from the right side of his head where it meets and links with the right hand, sit with your right knee hurdled and by the opponent's head and your left leg splayed to your rear, keeping the knee to the floor.

Pins: The Bedrock

To secure the hold lean forward and put your weight onto the opponent, to crank the neck, lean backwards and wrench the neck with the pull of both your arms. This is not a very strong hold (though on a good day with the wind behind you it can be) but it is an excellent mid-way point from upper 4 1/4 to mount. I personally use it more as a traveller's rest than anything else.

Defending the reverse scarf hold

There is not a lot that the opponent can do to escape from this position other than wriggle and thrash, if and when he does ride the storm, if he does look like escaping then move to a more prone position like the mount or the upper 4 1/4.

Attacking the reverse scarf hold

Whilst it is not easy for the opponent to escape from this position it is not the best place in the world to finish from either, quite often one has to move to a better position to secure a finish. Having said that the opponent's ribs, floating ribs in particular, are very vulnerable to strikes from the reverse scare hold, the throat is also very open to attacks from your right hand and the mount position is but the blink of an eye away, so better to use the scarf hold as a traveller's rest and do as much damage as possible whilst there, that way when, if, you do move to a better finishing position you will be dealing with a weakened, injured often exhausted opponent.

Chapter Six

Upper Four Quarter Hold Down

They say (who ever they are) that the best way to control a man is to control his head, then his body will follow. I have found this to be true both physically and psychologically, which is why the upper 4 1/4 is one of my favourite pins. It's not the prettiest of moves - in fact there is very little to get excited about when you look at the hold, perhaps that is why it is so often ignored. For me it is another real bread and butter pin, and if I get anyone that is too strong or who feels a little feisty or if I am feeling a little tired and need a rest then I'll whip around to the upper 4 1/4 at the earliest opportunity and control the opponent from the head down.

It is a very easy move to hold and a very hard move to escape from, a real wild and aggressive opponent will empty his fuel tank in a hurry when you hold him in the upper 4 1/4, also, if you position your body correctly, you can easily finish with a smother from this position and, if you desire you can get back to a standing position and finish from here also.

Upper 4 1/4 Hold down

Lie your chest on your opponent's head/face and straighten and splay your legs out directly behind you, grip his belt/trousers/ shirt (what ever you can grab) with both hands to secure the hold. To make the hold more uncomfortable for the opponent go on to your toes and focus your weight onto and through his face.

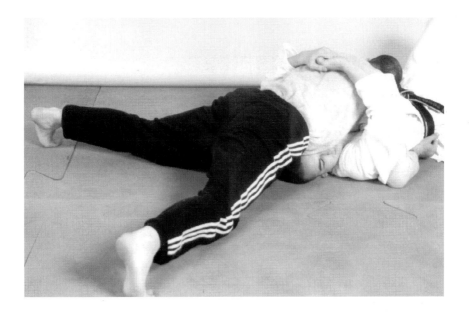

Pins: The Bedrock

Broken Upper 4 1/4 Hold down

A variation of this hold is to feed your arms under his, as opposed to over in the conventional hold, and grip the trousers, or even stagger the arms - one under his arm, one over. To be honest it doesn't really matter where your arms sit as long as you have a good grip and feel comfortable.

Knees Up

Upper 4 1/4 can also be employed with the knees up, as per illustration. This makes the hold more compact and is good preparation for movement-finish or standing up.

Pins: The Bedrock

Attacking the upper 4 1/4 Hold down.

The best attack from the upper 4 1/4 is the smother, force the opponent's face, via pain or pressure points, under the cheek bone, in the eye etc, so that it is facing upwards, lie your chest/ upper stomach across the nose and mouth to block the air ways and focus your weight onto and through the same point.

The groin is also open to hand strikes or grabs, it is also easy to feed your hands back and attack the throat and or larynx by squeezing it closed with one or both hands. The eyes can be attacked in the same way.

Defending the Upper 4 1/4 Hold down

Defence again is primarily about sensitivity, so go with the flow. If the opponent moves to the left, follow to the left, if he moves to the right, follow to the right, if he goes backwards or forwards then you do likewise. If you want to tire the opponent quickly give him some pain to trigger his in-fight adrenalin - but be ready for the possibility of bucking and bronking. The upper 4 1/4 is an ideal position for resting or for moving onto other positions for finish, ie the reverse scarf hold, mount position etc.

As with the other pins, flight time in holding, defending and attacking (from) the upper 4 1/4 is the pre-requisite to mastering it.

Chapter Seven

Drilling the Pins

The good thing about the pins is that you can quite easily, with practice, go from one to another and travel all around the body, allowing you to change pins according to the energy that your opponent feeds you.

It is also very disorientating to the opponent when you whiz around his body with consummate ease.

Changing from one pin to another needs to be smooth and practised so that, even though you are changing one hold for another, you are in no danger of losing the controlling position.

The first thing to address is drilling all of the pins in a sequence that takes you all around the body using all of the aforementioned pins, both left side and right side.

To start off with this routine should be done slowly and predictably so that all the tiny details are addressed. Later, after confidence in the holds has been found, you should practice going around the body without partner compliancy.

I am going to list some of the drills that I use and teach for ground pins but, as I always say, nothing is cast in stone and you can change the drills to suit or even make up drills of your own.

Eventually, with much flight time, you should feel as though you are floating from one pin to another - keeping body contact with him at all times - with the developed sensitivity you should feel as one with the opponent.

The 11 Pin drill

The 11 pin drill incorporates all of the pins in the latter pages from both left side and right (it is very important to be able to perform these moves from both sides). Because I have already gone through the finer details of the pins in the latter pages I will list the techniques in the following drill with no detail to technique. The pictures that illustrate will better show how to move from on technique to another.

Pins: The Bedrock

The Mount Position - Side 4 1/4 (right side)
- scarf hold (right side) - Jack-knife
- reverse scarf hold-upper 4 1/4 - jack-knife (left side)
- reverse scarf hold (left side) - scarf hold (left side)
- side 4 1/4 (left side) and back to the mount position.

Pins: The Bedrock

Pins: The Bedrock

Pins: The Bedrock

Keep practising with partner compliancy until you feel confident, then practice the individual pins without compliancy - it is important here that the opponent tries his hardest to escape - and ultimately the whole sequence with the opponent trying to escape at every and any opportunity.

Side to side drill

Right Scarf Hold - Mount position - left scarf Hold (see illus). Keep close to the opponent at all times, stick to him like glue and leave as little gap between you and him as possible as you go from one hold to another.

Pins: The Bedrock

Pins: The Bedrock

Scarf hold to jack-knife drill;
(practised to the left hand or/and right hand side)
Scarf hold - jack-knife.

As you move from the scarf hold to the jack-knife loosen the grip around his neck slightly and use your left hand to control his head, as you get into the jack-knife go straight onto your toes and focus all your weight onto your chest, which should be across his face, then jump back into the scarf hold again. Get a rhythm of going smoothly from scarf hold to jack-knife until your have done 10 repetitions of both holds.

Pins: The Bedrock

Jack-knife to upper 4 1/4 drill;
Jack-knife-Upper 4 1/4.

From the jack-knife position with your legs straight behind you and on your toes, release your grip around the opponent's head and move around, still on your toes so that the weight stays on the opponent, to the upper 4 1/4, as you move bring your arms down the torso of the opponent and grip an appendage to secure hold. Again move back and forward for 20 reps in all.

Pins: The Bedrock

Side to side drill;
Left side 4 1/4-mount-right side 4 1/4.

From the left side 4 1/4 pin crawl over the opponent's body into the mount position and then completely over into the right side 4 1/4 pin then move back the opposite way and repeat the exercise. Go over and back 20 times.

The fan drill; Right Side 4 1/4
- jack-knife - upper 4 1/4
- left jack-knife to left side 4 1/4.

Basically we are going all around the upper part of the opponent's body in a kind of fan action. From side 4 1/4 keep your legs straight and on your toes and quickly move right the way around the body going through right jack-knife to upper 4 1/4 to left jack-knife to left side 4 1/4 and then back again.

Stay on your toes and keep the movement light, almost hovering just above the opponent's body. Go back and forward twenty times using your hands to control the opponent's body on the way around.

Drills are very important if you want these techniques to work in the real world, so is un-compliancy on behalf of the opponent in training. As stated, all should be practised initially with a compliant opponent and then tested all-out with an opponent who is trying his utmost to escape.

If you do not practice in this way don't be surprised or disappointed when an un-compliant enemy throws you off like a piece of rag because you haven't pressure tested what you have. Pressure testing and un-compliancy will develop the right muscles and manipulative strength needed to make the technique real.

Conclusion

Thank you for reading Volume One of the ground fighting series, the pins are the bedrock. I have also given and hinted at some good finishes, although it goes without saying that control comes before finish if you want to be clinical. These moves need to be practised and re-practised diligently if you want your base to be a solid one to work from, as the great Musashi said (not to me personally): 1,000 days to learn technique, 10,000 days to polish.

These techniques are unlikely to work for you unless they become a part of you. The techniques that follow in the rest of the series, escapes and finishes of every kind, also only work on the premise that you have a good solid base from which to work. A finish without a base is like trying to put a gloss of paint over a lump of tree and call it furniture: priming is essential if you want a polished finish but, as they say (it's them again) you can't polish a turd, so at the very high risk of over emphasising the point and having people say 'my goodness that Geoff Thompson repeats himself a bit' get the basics right before moving onto the finishes or they'll be about as useful as something really useless.

Experiment, find and make moves up as you go along. As long as they work for you that's good enough. What you don't want to do is use filling techniques that look good but do not have a practical use. Rather, spend your time more constructively on the ones that really do and remember if there is no pressure then there is no guarantee.

For techniques on bars, chokes, strangles, fighting from the knees-back etc. please refer to the other five volumes advertised in the back of this text.

I wish you all the best with your search for better, more realistic fighting for defence. Knowledge is power: that knowledge can be derived from books, videos, courses, classes, practice etc.

Other books in this series:

GEOFF THOMPSON'S GROUND FIGHTING SERIES

THE ESCAPES

GROUND

GEOFF
THOMPSON

SUMMERSDALE

GEOFF THOMPSON'S GROUND FIGHTING SERIES

CHOKES AND STRANGLES

GEOFF THOMPSON

SUMMERSDALE

GEOFF THOMPSON'S GROUND FIGHTING SERIES

ARM BARS & JOINT LOCKS

GEOFF THOMPSON

SUMMERSDALE

GEOFF THOMPSON'S GROUND FIGHTING SERIES

FIGHTING FROM YOUR BACK

GEOFF THOMPSON

SUMMERSDALE

FIGHTING FROM YOUR KNEES

GEOFF THOMPSON

SUMMERSDALE

www.geoffthompson.com

www.summersdale.com